THE YOUNG LIFE OF POPE JOHN PAUL II

Claire Jordan Mohan

Illustrations

Jane Robbins

YOUNG SPARROW PRESS
P.O. Box 265 • Worcester, PA 19490
(215) 364-1945

Library of Congress Cataloging-in-Publication Data

Mohan, Claire Jordan
    The Young Life Of Pope John Paul II

SUMMARY: Describes the young life of Karol Cardinal Wojtyla of Poland, focusing on his boyhood years. Also details the influences of politics, history and religion that led to his great achievements. Included are his interests, hobbies and a discussion of the many obstacles he faced as a child and teenager. Clearly written, factual story.
    1. John Paul II. Pope. 1920– Juvenile literature.
    2. Popes – Biography – Juvenile literature.
    John Paul II. Pope 1920– 1. Title [B] [92] 2. Popes.

ISBN #0-943135-12-5 $7.95 paperback
ISBN #0-943135-11-7 $14.95 hard cover

CONTENTS

To my children
Bill, Trisha, Jan and Joann

"*Through the hands of such as yours God speaks, and from
behind your eyes he smiles upon the earth.*"

— *Kahil Gibran*

"Be not afraid to open your frontiers,
to open the doors of your life to Christ."

Pope John Paul II

PROLOGUE

There was a beautiful orange moon shining in the dark sky of early evening. The city of Rome was filled with excitement. The huge crowds stood outside the Sistine Chapel in the Piazza of San Pietro. The air of expectancy and tension was great. And then it was there — "white smoke" poured from the chimney, signaling that a new pope had been chosen.

Inside a strong silver-haired man sat alone at a table before the painting of Michaelangelo's Last Judgment. His head was in his hands. His body was slumped forward. The cardinals had been locked in for two days choosing the successor to Peter. It was October 16, 1978. Their choice had been made! It was the Polish Cardinal.

Karol Wojtyla seemed shocked. Despite the applause around him, he wept openly, his face in his hands. There was a long pause before he answered the life-changing question. Would he be the new pope? Finally he raised his head from his hands and replied "...placing my faith in God, I accept." His heart murmured, "Pray for me."

He knew somebody had to be the Pope yet he had never dreamed it would be he. He did not want the job. He had told his friends before he came that he would return to Krakow as soon as the choice of a new pope was made. Already he missed the mountains and lakes of Poland, the streets of his city.

His mind raced as he recalled the events of his life and the way he had been led by God to this moment. He remembered a lonely little boy and a day when sadness had overcome him.

1

AN ACHING HEART

◆ ◆ ◆

The day was cool and dark clouds loomed overhead. The young boy felt the darkness deep inside him. Nearby, there were weeping men and women silently huddled together like a wave of blackness before his eyes. He paid no attention to them. His eyes were focused ahead of him on a long rectangular object, so unfamiliar, yet compelling.

Young Karol, called "Lolek" by his family, clung tightly to the warm hand of the tall uniformed man next to him. His grief-filled father, who was wearing a black band around his sleeve, leaned over and put his arm around his son. "Lolek, we must be brave," he cautioned sadly. Tears rolled down the little lad's cheeks as he thought of his dear mother who would soon be gone from him in that deep cold grave.

He remembered her loving gentle face framed by dark curly hair, her warm eyes so proud of him, her comforting touch. He remembered the time he had fallen from the apple tree in the courtyard. How his head had ached! She ran to pick him up and touched his brow.

He wanted her to hold him again and hear her voice tell him, "Don't worry, my child, everything is going to be all right." He gasped as he held back his sobs.

The priest intoned the prayer he had heard often in church while serving as an altar boy at other funerals. Then, the words were for a stranger. Today was different. "The Lord is my shepherd...", he listened intently. As the psalm ended, the priest sprinkled holy water. Everyone walked slowly forward, like a line of ducklings following their mother. Each dropped a bright flower on the lonely box, until it was a quilt of many colors.

"But it won't keep her warm!" his heart silently screamed. As he watched spellbound, the wooden coffin slowly faded from his view as it was lowered into the deep dark hole.

A cool breeze caused him to shiver as the cries of his relatives rang in his ears. His kindly godmother put her arm around him, but he wanted to run away.

"I want my mother," he thought. "I can't leave her here all alone." His father grasped his hand and said, "Come, son, we must go home," and sadly he was led away. It was 1929 and Karol "Lolek" Wojtyla (voy-TEE-wah) was almost nine years old. The small boy thought, "My father is a retired army lieutenant. I must make him proud of me." He pulled back his shoulders and tried to stand erect with the military bearing of his father, just as his older brother, Edmund, was doing.

Edmund was already a man of twenty-one years of age and was studying medicine in a nearby town. Soon he would be a doctor. He would not be home to comfort his parent or brother. He had to leave that day. As they walked to the station, he whispered, "Lolek, take care of Papa. I'll try to get home often."

Patting his little brother on the head, he added, "You must write to me. Remember I love you and will help you all I can." Karol nodded his head and tearfully hugged him as the eerie whistle urged his brother to pick up his bag and board.

They waved a long good-bye as the train chugged out of the station and disappeared down the tracks. Karol and his father slowly and thoughtfully strode back to the empty gray house. As they neared the steps to enter, the door flew open and his little white dog, Bachik (baa-chick), dashed to his side. As it jumped up and licked him, the soft brown ears tickled his face. For a moment, the boy smiled.

2

MAMA, WE MISS YOU

◆ ◆ ◆

Sadly, they entered their second floor apartment. Karol's father pulled at his mustache and wiped the tears from his cheeks. Karol blinked his eyes and gazed around him. Home was not the same. It looked no different — the lace curtains, the velvet couch, the pictures on the wall, just as always. Yet, it was empty and silent.

Was it only a week ago that his pretty mother had happily taken him into the sunny parlor whispering her secret? Wasn't it only days ago that they had sat on the sofa as he learned that it was time for his baby brother or sister to be born? Was it only two days ago that a strange stoop-shouldered father had walked out of the bedroom with downcast eyes — eyes that told an unbearable message? His mama and a baby sister had died!

He thought of another night soon after his father had retired. He was sitting at the kitchen table doing his lessons. His mother was at the sink, singing as she broke string beans for the next day's dinner.

"Emilia, you sound like an angel," his father called from the sitting room where he was reading. "When you two are finished there, let's go for a walk. It is a beautiful night."

"That sounds good, dear," she replied. "Lolek is almost finished. Let's stop over at St. Mary's first. I want to light a candle."

He had finished his spelling homework and packed up his books. Then they were ready. First, they prayed at Our Lady's Shrine, then hand-in-hand, the three strolled down to the nearby park — a happy family together!

He remembered other rainy nights in that same room, sitting at his mother's side on the sofa. "Tell me about when you were young, Mama," he asked.

She looked at him warmly and told him what life was like when she was a little girl before the turn of the century. Mama loved to read to him, too. Her voice was soft and sweet. He could almost hear it now.

Lieutenant Wojtyla was also very sad and lonely without his dear wife who meant so much to him. Since Edmund was gone to be a doctor, father and son had only each other for consolation. They became almost like friends, as they shared not only their apartment, but also their daily work and play.

Their home was across the street from the beautiful Saint Mary's Church. The tall glowing tower dominated the horizon of their city and inspired Karol. The wide clock told him the time and Our Lady smiled at him from her statue above the door. Ever since the boy had been a little baby lying in his crib, he had heard the Angelus bells chiming. It was the first thing he remembered in his life.

The bells rang out their song at six in the morning and at six in the evening. They called all to pray and remember the time the Angel Gabriel had called on Mary and asked her to be the mother of God. He loved their song. They had always awakened him even before his mother's voice entered his room. "Lolek, it's time to get up." Every morning, now that there was just the two of them, the bells called him and his father to pray the Mass before he dashed off to school.

Often, in the days that followed his mother's death, his eyes would burn as he held back the tears that crept into them, even when he was in class. Karol attended the Wadowice Military School where boys wore military uniforms and hats and were taught to be little soldiers. Karol was proud to be like his father and brother—and big boys don't cry!

At first, it was hard for him to concentrate in school. As his dedicated teachers spoke, his thoughts were sometimes far away. He liked to daydream about his mother and the life he had before. She always wanted to know what he had learned and he delighted in relating the events of the day. Her memory was always a part of him. Sometimes an angry teacher would catch him and scold his distraction.

"Karol, you must pay attention, if you want to learn!" he would hear.

Usually, his teachers understood the pain in his heart.

"Little Karol needs our love now and in time he'll be the good student he always was. We must be patient with him," the principal was heard saying to the faculty.

Now, each evening, it was his father who would question him. "What did you do today? Do you like the academy?"

"You know, Papa," he answered, "I have to admit, I love school, especially the literature of Poland and the languages of other countries. Someday, I'll talk to people all over the world."

Then, while his father prepared the supper, Lolek did his homework or his chores of cleaning his room or sweeping the courtyard below.

3

HAPPIER DAYS

◆ ◆ ◆

Often the father and son would stroll the streets of the town, greeting their friendly neighbors and friends. Together they talked about his brother's success as a doctor or reminisced about Emilia and happier days.

The neighborhood boys were good friends. They knew Karol's sadness and tried to cheer him. After school, the boys came by his house and loudly called up to his second story window.

"Come on out, Karol, let's play some soccer." This lad loved the game and couldn't wait to play.

"I'm on my way," he replied.

Quickly, he would finish his tasks, grab the ball, and with Bachik at his heels, join them. For a while his joy in the game would take all of his attention. As the goal keeper, he couldn't think of anything else during the active game. Even his dog had to sit quietly on the sidelines or he was banished by his master.

Even so, trouble sometimes followed him. There were no playgrounds in that town. The game was on the street—and the street was next to the church. As they played, with their minds only on the game, the ball would slam against the wall of the church.

"What are you boys doing?" an angry priest, interrupted at prayer, would shout at them. "Boys, I've told you before, I'm not telling you again. Don't play here. Go somewhere else."

They would move down the street that day, but boys have been known to ignore warnings and many times they saw the priest again as he ran out the sturdy church door with his black cassock flying and reprimanded them for forgetting.

Time did not stand still. Life for Karol and his father gradually brought light-hearted times. Summer came like a shining beam. School was out and the two were called away from their deep sorrow. Karol's unhappy moments became less and less. He was a little boy. The father knew that they had to go on. He told his son, "Lolek, we cannot forget mama, but she would not want us to be sad."

One bright morning, Lieutenant Wojtyla awoke Karol, "Lolek, the golden sunshine calls through my open window. Let's take the canoe down the river. Mama is not here to pack us a lunch, but we still have each other and we must thank God for that." "Oh, Papa, that sounds great. I'll be ready in a minute," he replied.

That was the beginning. Soon they enjoyed many activities together. This young boy was an outdoors type of kid. He loved any activities associated with nature. In the summer he was called by the dark green forests where he hiked for hours. He swam daily in the cool waters of the mountain-fed river nearby. Whether he was alone or with others, he could never get enough of God's wonderful world!

The snow-covered mountains drew him and the winter was his favorite season. His friends laughed at his love to ski even on the coldest days. One day, his shivering friend who was ready to leave for a nice warm fire, questioned him.

"Hey, Karol, what can you like so much about this frigid weather?"

"I don't know exactly. It's just I like to feel the swish of the snow beneath my feet and the cold air on my face. And besides that, it means I can go skiing and you know how I love that!" he replied and he was out on the slopes of the wonderful hills around his city almost every day.

4

A NEW INTEREST

◆ ◆ ◆

It was not just sports that called to this young lad. Karol had many other talents that would remain with him for years. Since he was a little shy, he liked to playact whenever the chance came up in school. He felt at home doing this and everyone recognized his skill.

His teacher or other students said, "Karol, you would be perfect for this part!"

"Sounds good to me," he answered. "Tell me about it."

Soon he was known as a convincing actor both in elementary school and later on in high school where he starred in many plays. He had a quiet way and was not a show-off type of kid. He did not offend others or make them envy him and he always had a lot of fun.

Singing and folk-dancing were a way of life in this world without television shows, or exciting computer games back in the 1930's.

"I love to sing and dance," he told all who would listen and all the town girls wanted to be his partner. They liked his good-natured cheerful ways. Not only that, but his dark brown hair falling across his deep-set eyes, his neat clothes, and his dancing feet gave him a look they couldn't resist.

The prettiest schoolgirls would wish, "I hope Lolek is my partner," as they met in the town square every week. Yet, shy Karol knew nothing of this.

Days were not always carefree. One afternoon when he was twelve, tragedy again struck the Wojtyla family. Father and son were in the courtyard playfully tossing a ball to Bachik. They laughed happily at his antics and patted his head as he returned with his prize. "Good boy," they pronounced. Suddenly, they heard the screech of bicycle tires and glanced toward the street. Coming toward them was the cyclist delivering a telegram.

"Telegrams usually mean bad news, don't they, Papa?" Karol asked anxiously.

Lieutenant Wojytla's hand shook as he tore open the yellow envelope.

"What does it say, Papa?" the worried boy questioned.

Tears streamed from his father's eyes. "God be with us, Lolek," he answered gravely. "Edmund has died! Scarlet fever has killed him!" He hugged his son. Together they wept.

The news spread throughout their town. Neighbors offered help. Lolek's friends gathered in the courtyard. "What happened, Karol" they asked.

"There was a scarlet fever epidemic. Edmund caught it from one of his patients. Oh, I can't believe it," he replied. "My brother was a doctor and doctors,

doctors don't die—they help people to live!" Sadly, he added, "He was supposed to come home this weekend. We've already made plans."

The boys tried to comfort him in their own ways, but he was desolate. He was twelve years old. Three years ago his mother had died, now this. Edmund was not only his brother, he was his hero.

Somehow they got through the funeral and it was back to school for Lolek. There, his teachers noted how sad-eyed and serious he had become.

"What's wrong with Karol?" they questioned each other. "He does not seem himself and his mind is not on his work."

When they discovered the reason, they knew that for now, Karol could only think about Edmund and muse that his brother would never come home again.

5

IMPORTANT DECISIONS

◆ ◆ ◆

Gradually Karol's spirits revived and school work helped heal his heart. Something about poetry fascinated him. He especially liked to read about his native land of Poland. He even wrote some poems himself. His father encouraged him and his opinion was important to his son.

"What do you think of this, Papa?" he questioned after he carefully read the words he had written.

"I think it is fine, son. Keep at it," was the usual honest reply.

Karol's talents and love of study paid off. As the years passed and he went to high school, he became one of the top students in town. In Poland, everyone must take a school-leaving exam and he was at the top of his class.

One morning in early spring just before graduation, father and son were sitting in their sunny kitchen eating their breakfast of potato pancakes and tripe. His father suddenly pushed back his chair and walked over to put his hand on his son's shoulder.

"I am so proud of you, Lolek," he said. "Your mother must be, too. I have been thinking of something and I want to hear your thoughts on it."

"Sure, Papa, what is it?"

"Well, son, you love literature, poetry and the theater so much, I think we should move to Krakow so you can study at the Jagiellonian University. Your mother's family has a little house in that city. There is no reason we can't leave Wadowice."

"Papa, I would love that," he replied happily.

It was nine years since the saddest day of his life and six years since scarlet fever had caused the death of his brother. Karol could hardly believe the words his father spoke. He really wanted to go to the university.

He thought, "A change will be good for both of us. It is just my papa and I now and time for a new life."

"How soon can we leave?" he asked.

Shortly after this, the archbishop of Krakow came to Karol's high school. The brightest boy was chosen to greet the bishop. It was Karol.

After the greeting, the archbishop asked the boy, "Well, young man, what are you planning to do with your life?"

"I will be going to the Jagiellonian University in September, Father," he replied "I plan on studying Polish literature."

"My son, that is a wonderful university and I'm sure you will do very well. Polish literature, you say. Do you like to write?"

"Oh yes, Your Eminence" he answered. "I have been writing since I was little."

"Well," said the archbishop, "I hear you are not only a good student, but come from a very holy family. God bless you."

Turning to the principal of the school, and shaking his head, the archbishop said, "What a fine young lad. Too bad he has other plans. We could do with someone like him in the Church."

Silently, Karol pondered what he had heard.

"Well," he thought, "I know my mama would have loved me to serve God that way. Papa would be proud, too. But somehow I can't see myself as a priest. I do love God, but I will serve him some other way."

6

WAR COMES TO POLAND

◆ ◆ ◆

World events would change the course of his life, but it was 1938 and no dark clouds hung over him, yet. For a year Karol not only studied at the university, but also became a part of the Rhapsodic Theater.

Karol and his friends founded a student group, "Studio 39." The students wrote, staged, and performed their own plays. The form of acting was different from what he was used to and he was eager to learn. The actors did not use scenery or action, but would say their lines in front of a dark curtain. Sometimes they would use a prop or two; sometimes they would dress the part of the character they were portraying. It was a new experience and one this young man really enjoyed.

And then, World War II darkened the sky of Poland in 1939. After the Germans came, the theater could no longer operate as before. This did not stop the dedicated group. They went underground and performed secretly in homes around the city. The dramas were filled with patriotic sentiments and were used to stiffen the morale of the Polish people. These helped keep alive a flicker of hope.

It was on September 1, 1939 that the German armies crossed the Polish frontier and launched an attack which immediately shattered the peace. By the end of the month, Poland had ceased to exist! The so-called German blitzkrieg deployed highly armored tanks, trucks, and self-propelled guns through Poland's front lines.

Within two days, German forces had sealed off the Polish Corridor and were converging on the city of Krakow. By the end of the second week, the Polish army was defeated and Poland was no longer free. The whole country was occupied by the Germans and they were in total control.

Life totally changed for the people of Poland when their country was invaded. Churches were taken over, universities were closed, and everyone lived in fear of the Germans.

Karol was no longer a student, although he studied on his own. He was ordered to work at a limestone factory where the labor was hard, the hours were very long, and the factory was open night and day. Karol felt lucky when he was on the night shift. On those occasions, once the deliveries were made, he could spend his time reading.

In the terrible years of the Occupation, no one knew when they left for school in the morning or went to work, whether they would see each other at supper that evening. Each day, for all they knew, could be their last. Police round-ups, deportation to camps, forced labor in Germany, death by shooting on the street—all these things were part of daily life. Any night the Gestapo might turn up, batter down the door and drag someone off to prison or straight to the Auschwitz concentration camp. Shots were heard at night when the police arrested people caught walking the streets and fired at any who did not stop. Everywhere was a state of constant terror and intimidation — and Karol's life was a part of this.

7

ANOTHER TRAGIC LOSS

◆ ◆ ◆

During this fearful time, when he worked the day shift, the son came home for lunch with his father. Both of them looked forward to this time.

"Papa, it is good for us to talk and be together. Who knows what will happen these days," he wondered.

One day, no different from the others, Karol returned home happily expecting to get his father's opinion on what was going on. What he found was his father lying quietly—too quietly—on the brown leather couch.

"Papa, what's wrong?" he cried.

It was a heart attack. At first, Karol could not believe it. His beloved father was dead!

"Please, just be asleep, Papa," he begged as the truth sunk in.

For twelve hours he stayed at his father's side praying. A tall candle burned by the bed. It reminded him of the brief flicker that was life. The darkened room and the crucifix on the wall calmed him and eased his grief.

Soon the church bells tolled calling all to pray—another soul had gone to God. With the company of a few friends and neighbors, he walked slowly behind the brown box into the open doors of the church. The priest intoned the familiar words and Karol's eyes filled with tears. This time there was no one who could comfort him. Karol was truly alone.

His mother was gone, his brother was gone, now his father was gone, and the world was in turmoil. Events like these could harden many a heart. Karol, rather, missing the one who had always been beside him, turned to his Eternal Father for solace.

His religion meant more and more to him. Eventually, he met up with some new friends like himself and became part of a "living rosary" group of young men. They would meet to read the Scriptures, attend Mass, and pray together.

In their world, the atmosphere of hatred and vengefulness toward the enemy was becoming more intense. Small boys dreamt of armed retaliation for the wrongs and humiliation of their country and the murder of their parents, brothers, and sisters. The rosary group attempted to overcome this hatred. They concerned themselves with modeling their character on that of Christ.

Though they were not part of the Resistance group who secretly defied the enemy, they worried that at any moment the Gestapo might get wind of their meetings and pack them off to concentration camps.

The Germans would never believe these secret meetings were purely for religious purposes.

Karol, and his friends, especially Mietek, a young fellow with whom he became close, often talked about the future and their preparations for the work of rebuilding their country. They pondered how they could best help their land and its people after the war was over.

8
ANANSWERING A CALL
♦ ♦ ♦

During this time, Karol was still acting in the home theater and loving it. He was also doing a lot of thinking about himself. He knew he was old enough to make major changes in his life. He was torn and felt it was time for him to make basic decisions.

"Should I make a career of acting? Is that what I am called to do?—or should I go on to something else?" he questioned himself.

The day finally came when he made up his mind. Life was still crazy in Poland, but he had found his answer. His decision made, he looked for his friend and found him on the narrow street where he lived with his mother, sister, and brother.

"Mietek, I am going up to Warsaw, would you like to come with me?" he asked.

"Sure, Karol, what's up?" asked Mietek.

"I want to visit a priest I knew when I was little back in Wadowice."

"Okay, I'm free right now, let's go," he replied.

They checked the schedule and were off on the next train. When they arrived in the city, they walked till they came to a large gray castle guarded by the German police.

"This is it," said Karol.

After showing the police their credentials, they were allowed to enter. They walked up a flight of broad, highly-polished wooden stairs. At the top they met the cheerful-looking priest. They went into a bright sparsely furnished parlor.

"How about some tea?" he asked. "You must be tired after your long trip."

They agreed and were served the hot tea and some pastry.

After some conversation with the two young men, the priest said, "Well, Karol, let's go off by ourselves for a bit. Mietek, we won't be long."

Mietek picked out a comfortable chair by the window, looked out for a while, then settled down to read the Bible which was on a nearby table. It was not a "little while." Mietek began to wonder what was going on.

When his friend finally returned, it was almost time for their train to leave. After saying, "I'll see you soon," to the priest, Karol and his friend started on their way home. Mietek waited until they were seated on the train.

Then he questioned, "Karol, tell me. Why were you talking so long? What's going on?"

Karol stopped and looked at him steadily, but did not seem to hear the question. He simply said, "I've wanted to tell you something, Mietek. I have decided to become a priest."

Mietek looked back at him and replied, "Karol, I guess I already knew that."

Very soon, after getting his affairs in order, his possessions stored, and his bags packed, Karol went off to a secret seminary hidden from the enemy. There he learned theology by night and prepared for the priesthood, although he still had to work in the factory by day. In time the Germans were defeated, World War II was finally over, and now the Communists took over Poland.

Karol studied very hard for several years. He did learn to speak many more languages, and he did become a priest in 1946 — but that is not all. He was quickly recognized as a man of God and went from priest to bishop to cardinal.

9

A NEW POPE

◆ ◆ ◆

Finally, at 6:10 P.M. on Monday, October 16, 1978, two weeks after the sudden death of Pope John Paul, the College of Cardinals chose him as the Church leader and successor to Christ himself. A puff of white smoke exiting from the Vatican smokestack told all the world that a selection had been made.

One hour later, as men and woman from all over the world watched impatiently, a figure appeared on the Papal balcony.

"We have a pope," he announced amid cheers. "His name is Carolum Wojtyla..."

The crowd was startled. "Who is this?" they wondered. "He is not an Italian!" "All popes have been from Italy for over four hundred years." "Where is he from?" "We have never heard this name." These were questions asked throughout the plaza.

Silently, the disappointed spectators looked at each other in bewilderment. All was strangely quiet until minutes later when Karol appeared on the balcony and astonished his audience by speaking to them in perfect Italian. Suddenly, a smiling crowd of thousands cheered.

Karol, now known as Pope John Paul II, is still fond of hiking, swimming, and skiing, but God's work is keeping him busy with more important things today. Rather than guiding others along the snowy slopes, he continually guides their souls along the trails of life. His goal is to insure their journey ends not at the base of a silver mountain, but before the Golden Gates of Heaven.

CHRONOLOGY

◆ ◆ ◆

1920   Born Karol Jozef Wojtyla in Wadowice,
        Poland on May 18.

1920   Baptized at St. Mary's Church in Wadowice
        on June 20.

1929   Mother, Emilia, died in childbirth.

1932   Brother, Edmund, died of scarlet fever
        in December.

1938   Karol, Jr. passes high school leaving exams
        and he and his father moved to Krakow. He
        entered the Jagiellonian University.

1939   Karol and his friends founded
        "Studio 39".

1939   Poland is invaded by the Germans.

1941   Father, Karol Sr., died in Krakow.

1942   Karol entered underground seminary to study
        by night.

1944   August 6 Gestapo arrested all males
        age 15 to 50.
        Karol escapes to Palace Seminary.

1945   Krakow is liberated by Russian Army
        in January.

1946   Karol is ordained a priest on November 1.

1958   Karol is consecrated auxiliary bishop of
        Krakow, September 28.

1963	Karol is appointed archbishop on December 30.
1967	Karol is named cardinal by Pope Paul VI on May 9.
1978	Albino Luciani was named Pope John Paul I on August 6.
1978	Pope John Paul I died after 33 days in office on September 28.
1978	Cardinals are locked in to choose successor of Pope John Paul I on October 14.
1978	Karol is chosen as the new pope. He took name John Paul II on October 16.
1978	Inauguration Mass is celebrated on October 22.

QUOTATIONS

◆ ◆ ◆

"To attain to this which you know not you must pass through that which you know not. To attain to this which you possess not you must pass through that which you possess not. To attain this which you are not you must pass through that which you are not."

St. John of the Cross

"Hands are the heart's landscape. They split sometimes like ravines into which an undefined force rolls. The very same hands that a man only opens when his palms have had their fill of toil. Now he sees; because of him others walk in peace."

"The Quarry" Karol Wojtyla

"Things eternal, things of God, are very simple and very profound. We don't have to create new programs; we have to find new ways, new energies, and a new enthusiasm for sharing in the eternal plan of God, and of fulfilling it in the context of our times."

Karol Wojtyla on occasion of his
consecration as archbishop,
March 8, 1964

"Together we were called to God's vineyard to do his work long, long ago. We know the value and the price of each and every human life... We know it, because we have heard his call: Let us shape our life according to the gospel. Let us give the Gospel the shape of our own life — though the attempt be difficult and awkward."

Sermon September 24, 1978
Cathedral of Our Lady, Munich

"Let each one of you consider his own life. Am I prudent? Do I live consistently and responsibly? Does the programme I am realizing serve the real good? Does it serve the salvation that Christ and the Church want for us? I, the Pope, who am speaking to you, must also consider what I must do to live prudently."

Pope John Paul II, Oct. 25, 1978

"To the see of Peter in Rome there succeeds today a bishop who is not a Roman. A bishop who is a son of Poland. But from this moment he too becomes a Roman."

Pope John Paul II, Oct. 22, 1978

"May Jesus Christ be praised. Dearest brothers and sisters, we are still all grieved after the death of the most beloved Pope John Paul I.

"And now the most reverend cardinals have called a new bishop of Rome. They have called him from a distant country, distant but always so close for the communion in the Christian faith and tradition.

"I was afraid to receive this nomination, but I did it in the spirit of obedience to Our Lord and in the total confidence in his mother, the most holy Madonna.

"Even if I cannot explain myself well in your — our — Italian language, if I make a mistake you will correct me.

"And so I present myself to you all to confess our common faith, our hope, our confidence in the mother of Christ and the church, and also, to start anew on that road, the road of history and of the church — to start with the help of God and with the help of men."

Pope John Paul II, Oct. 22, 1978

"What is the fate the Lord has in store for his Church in the next years? And what path will humanity take, as it draws near to the year 2000? These are difficult questions, to which we can only reply: God knows."

Pope John Paul II

"Whatever you wish that men would do to you, so do to them."

Pope John Paul II

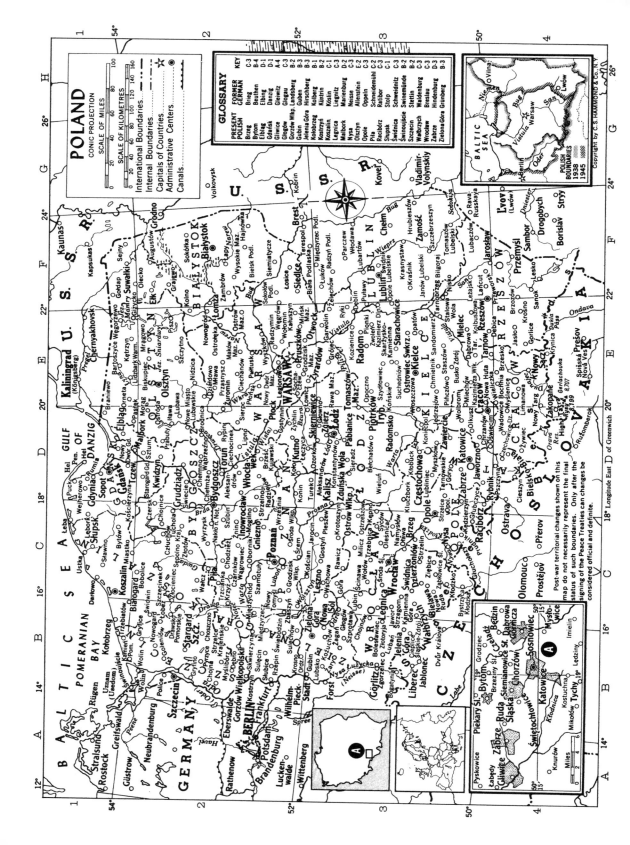

FURTHER READING

◆ ◆ ◆

Douglas, Robert. *John Paul, The Pilgrim Pope*. Chicago: Children's Press, 1980 .

Frossard, Andre and Pope John Paul II. *"Be Not Afraid."* New York: St. Martin's Press, 1984.

Greeley, Andrew M. *The Politics of Intrigue in the Vatican*. Kansas City: Andrews and McMeel, Inc., 1979.

Hebblethwaite, Peter. *The Year of Three Popes*. Cleveland- New York: William Collins, Inc., 1979.

Hebblethwaite, Peter and Kaufmann, Ludwig. *John Paul II A Pictorial Biography*. New York: McGraw-Hill Book Co. 1979.

Heiferman, Ronald. *World War II*. London: Octopus Books Ltd. 1973 .

Malinski, Mieczyslaw. *Pope John Paul II, The Life of Karol Wojtyla*. New York: The Seabury Press, 1979.

Oram, Jame. *The People's Pope, The Story of Karol Wojtyla of Poland*. San Francisco: Chronicle Books, 1979 .

Wynn, Wilton. *Keeper of the Keys*. New York: Random House, 1988 .

Wojtyla, Karol. *Easter Vigil & Other Poems*. New York: Random House, 1979.

Wojytla, Karol. *The Jeweler's Shop*. New York: Random House, 1980 .

GLOSSARY

◆ ◆ ◆

Altar boy – a boy who assists the celebrant at a church service.

Angelus Bells – bells that announce the story of the Angel Gabriel's appearance to Mary as he asked her to be the mother of God.

Archbishop – a bishop of high rank.

Armed retaliation – to get revenge by use of guns and ammunition.

Auschwitz Concentration Camp – a place of suffering to which the German s sent their supposed enemies.

Bachik – (baa-chick) a Polish word meaning "little shepherd."

Basic decisions – important decisions about one's life.

Bible – the sacred scriptures of Christians comprising the Old and New Testaments.

Bishop – a member of the clergy ranking above a priest.

Black arm band – a black band worn to express grief at the death of a loved one.

Blitzkrieg – a sudden violent enemy attack.

Cardinal – an official of the Roman Catholic Church ranking next below the Pope.

Clergy – a body of religious officials authorized to conduct services.

College of Cardinals – the group of cardinals who advise the Pope and who meet to elect a new pope at the death of the reigning pope.

Courtyard – an enclosure next to a building.

Credentials – something such as identification papers that gives a basis for confidence.

Deportation – banishment.

Eternal Father – God, the Creator of the world.

Faculty – the teachers in a school or college.

German army – the military forces of Germany.

Gestapo – a terrorist secret police organization in Germany operating against persons suspected of disloyalty to their country.

Heart attack – heart disease due to an insufficient blood supply to the heart muscle.

Lieutenant – a commissioned officer in military service.

Light a candle – a ritual of the Roman Catholic Church in which the lighting of a candle represents a prayer.

Mass – a sequence of prayers and ceremonies of the Roman Catholic Church representing the Last Supper of Jesus.

Occupation – the taking possession of an area by foreign military forces.

Piazza of San Pietro – the plaza at St. Peter's Basilica in Rome, Italy.

Poland – a country in eastern Europe east of Germany, west of Russia, north of Czechoslovakia, south of the Baltic Sea.

Polish frontier – the border of Poland.

Pope – the head of the Roman Catholic Church.

Priest – a person having the authority to perform the sacred rites of a religion.

Resistance group – a group resisting the authority of the Germans in World War II.

Rosary – a string of beads used in prayer and meditation.

Scarlet fever – a highly contagious disease marked by fever, sore throat and a red rash.

Scriptures – the books of the Bible.

Seminary – an educational institution that gives theological training.

Telegram – a message sent by code over wires.

Theology – the study of religious faith, practice, and experience; the study of God and God's relation to the world.

Tripe – the stomach tissue of an animal, often an ox, used as food.

World in turmoil – the world in an extremely confused and agitated condition.

INDEX

ABOUT THE AUTHOR

◆ ◆ ◆

CLAIRE JORDAN MOHAN, formerly of King of Prussia and Lansdale, now resides in Chalfont, Pennsylvania with her husband, Robert. Having retired from full-time teaching at Visitation B.V.M. School in Trooper, PA, she spends her time writing, painting and traveling.

She has had many articles published in magazines and newspapers and has appeared on national radio and television shows, including Mother Angelica Live, the 700 Club and CNBC. On a recent trip to Rome for the Beatification of Blessed Frances Siedliska, Claire Mohan presented a special edition of her book to Pope John Paul II.

She is the mother of five children and grandmother of twelve. Claire is a graduate of Little Flower High School and is a 1984 summa cum laude graduate of Villanova University where she was valedictorian of her class. She attended Chestnut Hill College for graduate studies. Claire Jordan Mohan welcomes interviews and speaking engagements.

ABOUT THE ILLUSTRATOR

◆ ◆ ◆

JANE ROBBINS' clean, sharp illustrations reflect her classical training. An art major in high school, she was awarded a scholarship to Moore College of Art. She studied at Philadelphia College of Art, and Fleisher's Memorial in Philadelphia, Baum School in Allentown, and Bishop University in Quebec. She taught painting at the YWCA in Philadelphia and has held private art classes in her Red Hill, Pennsylvania home. In addition to Claire Mohan's current book, Mrs. Robbins illustrated "Redheads" and has written and illustrated articles for magazines. The winner of numerous awards, her work is in private collections throughout the United States and Canada.

OTHER BOOKS

by Claire Jordan Mohan

◆ ◆ ◆

Mother Teresa's Someday

School children delight in this beautifully illustrated story that tells the details of Mother Teresa's young life as a child in Yugoslavia. This account of her childhood is filled with joyful family experiences shared with her parents, brother and sister.

A Red Rose for Frania

This children's book offers young readers a thoughtful endearing story of Frances Siedliska's joys and struggles on her pathway to sainthood.

This story demonstrates courage and perseverance as it describes Frania's poor health and obstacles in committing to religious life.

Kaze's True Home

This delightful story of the young life Maria Kaupas will inspire each child as young Casimira follows her star to attain "the impossible dream." "Kaze" as she was called, was neither wealthy nor did she enjoy the opportunities of the young people of today, but she loved God and was able to share her love with others.

Young Sparrow Press • Box 265 • Worcester, PA 19490

WHAT OTHERS ARE SAYING ABOUT
The Young Life of Pope John Paul II

◆ ◆ ◆

"I am confident that our young people and their parents and teachers will find this work an enjoyable and valuable resource." — Anthony Cardinal Bevilacqua, Archbishop of Philadelphia

"I was impressed with your ability to tell his story with conviction, sincerity and with true emotion. I was indeed caught up in the biography you have written for young people." — Yvonne S. Walther, Former Associate Editor, Junior Books, Westminster Press; E.P. Dutton; and Harper & Row

"How the Pope handled the trials and triumphs of his boyhood... is one that will encourage children in the attempt to imitate the characteristics which made this man one to admire and emulate... How he dealt with the tragedies of his life are told in this inspiring story." — NARÓD POLSKI, Official Publication of the Polish Catholic Union of America